T0195935

THE ALPHA ALCHEMY

Grounded in Grace

LINDY LEWIS

BALBOA.PRESS

A DIVISION OF HAY HOUSE

Balboa Press books may be ordered through booksellers or by contacting:

Balboa Press
A Division of Hay House
1663 Liberty Drive
Bloomington, IN 47403
www.balboapress.com
1 (877) 407-4847

Book Design: Emerald Dumas

Photographs: Marie-Dominique Verdier

Print information available on the last page.

ISBN: 978-1-9822-4182-7 (sc)
ISBN: 978-1-9822-4183-4 (e)

Library of Congress Control Number: 2020901157

Balboa Press rev. date: 04/14/2020

"Lindy's advice and insight affirms to a confused twenty-something (me) that with soft awareness, I CAN beat the Self-Defeating Cycle. Her strength, vulnerability and power of voice serve as an inspiring catalyst for self-change.

I will take her voice with me as I move into a lifestyle of truly implementing Grace, learning to let go of Expectations (future resentments) and walking fluidly into a Faith-Forward journey."

- Courtney, a tenacious & exhausted soul-searching female

Grounded in Grace and Gratitude

In every endeavor, I strive to remain grounded
in gratitude for those around me. I am eternally
grateful to my fellow Alpha females of all ages that
have found this work useful in their own lives.

My children, Jerry, Cia, and John Hanford,
and their children, are the reason I truly show
up so honest, vulnerable, and authentic.

I have found that when peace returns to
'her' soul, she will find health, happiness,
and more than she could have dreamt.

In creating the Inspiring Grace series, I have come
to recognize that it is likewise imperative to extend
gratitude for one's own contributions to a healthier self.
I am constantly reminded to appreciate the value in this
dance and gentle balance of the Alpha and Omega.

Introduction

MY WHY

For six months this book sat patiently waiting for my stamp of approval as I've hemmed and hawed, slowly searching for the perfect introduction to inspire and engage the Alpha Female to slow down before her health, family, and overscheduled world blows!! I was **Stuck in the Muck** until I reminded myself that I, too, am recovering, not recovered. I am on this journey with you, learning, growing, creating a new identity, and authenticating myself. The **Ah-has** I am promoting are won through practice and the daily resolve to continue my own health and healing journey.

My hope is to compel the Type A, busy-all-day, externally driven, perfectionist seeker to slow down so that she can receive the wisdom of this book. By heeding the persistent heart whispers, you can prevent yourself from getting taken out sideways by dis-ease, divorce, depression or any other labels. This is the hard road and could simply be brushed aside as you plow through continuing to achieve, accomplish, and live up to expectations you've placed on yourself. However, succumbing to the alpha's determination will put you at risk of losing yourself, your health, and your tribe.

We drone on, numb out, check the heartless checklist, ignore our gut wisdom, as we wear our overachieving, Type A, accomplished state like a badge of honor. This badge gains us kudos, respect, credit, accolades, and motivates us to keep forcing forward. However, there is no honorary badge for all of these accomplishments and feats; instead, there is overwhelm, loss of connection, and exhaustion to the core. As the societal bar continues to rise right alongside our own, beware that this aim and drive is a crash course.

So why is it so important to slow, soften, and choose a **walk of Grace?** It's freeing and liberating to come from self-acceptance and self compassion. Living my Lingo maintains that sweet balanced spot in life – **the Alpha Alchemy!** These **Ah-has** are simple, practical, and purposeful tools that offer permission and can shift your perspective. Loosening the rigid Alpha edges enables you to trust your guide inside. This book series is a colorful and empowering journey to help you navigate and unwind your mind while nourishing your relationship with self and others. This mindset of discovery and curiosity grounds your **Goddess in Grace.**

So, here's my best pitch for your mind, body, and spirit, ladies… Let go of those expectations and dive deep to reconnect with your true, **YOUnique**, authentic selves as your quality of life and love depends on it.

WHAT LIES WITHIN

The Journey Continues:

Foreword:

WHY AM I DOING THIS?

Alchemy: /alkəmē/ n. *Transforming things for the better; a seemingly magical process of transformation, creation, or the combination; often in a way that cannot be explained.*

Why am I doing this? That question often finds me unsuspecting. Whether I'm running into an old friend at the post office or I'm home alone quietly **Zentering** myself by the fire, it will sneak up and tap me on the shoulder. "Hey, Lindy. Why?" Why the books and stickers? Why the peace rings? Why the road trips to book signings and the energy into the nonprofit? After all, with a body that hosts the disease MS, I am tired and often drained. So why do I persevere with this movement to help myself and others recover from our Alpha Female ways?

Truly, my answer is that **Grace** is a calling. It is my calling. I am here to encourage, enliven, and empower women to trust their heart whispers. While I hope there is much to learn from

I AM HERE TO ENCOURAGE, ENLIVEN, AND EMPOWER WOMEN

these three volumes, as well as to practice with the follow-up **Grace Guide**, I tend to think of my books as being about *inspiration*, not *information*. The aim is to provide the insights that will help others on the path to their own place of Grace, because no matter your profession or lifestyle, the world needs you to come forth yielding your softness and a sense of unconditional acceptance. While I enthusiastically offer guidance, **Grace** is not something that I can give you. It's not something attainable outside of yourself, rather it requires you to **Bring it Yin.**

GRACE IS NOT SOMETHING I CAN GIVE YOU

And, yes, I also do it for myself. I do it for my self-health, in fact. Everything that I am sharing with you throughout the entire *Inspiring Grace* series is something that I have done. It's something that I still do. Each day, I dance the **Ah-has** as a testament to the fact that I recognize the paradox of needing both sides of my Alpha personality. These are the means by which to balance that duality. They aren't just something for me to write about, rather, they are skills that are practiced again and again in an ongoing journey to Align the Alpha.

Self-acceptance and self-love are the fruits of engaging in reflection, rather than reaction. They are refined and strengthened as we embrace our shadow side, as we **hold space** for both our light and our darkness. And when we love and accept ourselves unconditionally, something else naturally follows. Without fear or force, this **Grace** we find is able to ripple out where it touches and changes our families, our relationships, and our communities.

My dream for you is that these books will help you discover a new language that resonates within – that you will find a new perspective and a new way of communicating with yourself that leads to better health and happiness. It may seem a small thing to **Find Someone as Normal as You,** to **Cancel the Comparative Narrative,** or to tell yourself that your **Quirks Make You Colorful,** but each helps hold you on your journey. We need more Alphas on Purpose in this world. Rather than being distracted or caught in the **Frenetic Energetic,** you can develop the ability to Alpha Up only when it's useful to you. When you set your intentions and use your feminine power for its highest purpose, you will find yourself able to rise strong with the vision of an eagle who is able to take in a comprehensive view while remaining unaffected by what it sees.

DEVELOP THE ABILITY TO ALPHA UP

Becoming an entrepreneur and a catalyst for change offers its challenges. I choose to take the high road, which all too often feels like opting for the hard road. It is not always easy to choose real, raw, unconditional self-acceptance. However, holding space for myself and others to join and stay in this walk has yielded bountiful rewards. It is such an honor to be a guide and witness as others are inspired to transform their **quirks** into their colors, to recognize that each is a beautiful, **YOUnique** part of their own authentic spirit of expression.

INVOKING GRACE IS LIVING THE ALPHA'S ALCHEMY

Let's get the bad news out of the way, first: There's a pretty good chance you're contributing to the Alpha Addiction. Perhaps you are numbing the senses by winding down with a bottle of red wine in the evening. Or maybe you're staying late at work to perfect a presentation. Neither of these is necessarily a problem, but they're not necessarily not a problem, either. It's when they are a means to avoid being with yourself and your thoughts that things start to get worrisome.

I've previously referred to the Alpha Addiction as an epidemic; and while I still hold that to be true, one of my wise **Youngers** recently expanded my perception of the concept. I had been viewing this type of large-scale self-avoidance as a numbing of the world. I was so focused on that enormous, big picture that I overlooked the fact that it is a devastating force on an individual level, too. Addiction – not just in terms of substance abuse – is a pattern that keeps you from being with yourself. It is a means to avoid your own feelings and emotions. It provides an alternative to being alone with your own sad, scary, and overwhelming thoughts. Unfortunately, we're passing these patterns on.

ADDICTION IS A PATTERN THAT KEEPS YOU FROM BEING WITH YOURSELF

Despite the fact that we don't need more **Alpha-holics** in the world, we sure do seem to be turning out a lot of Type-A personalities. Our **Youngers** are being told daily that their worth is defined by external accomplishments. They are constantly cajoled to strive for the trophies, the grades, the accolades, and the money. Unfortunately, when your self-perception is based on external validation, things can get pretty rough when the affirmations and "atta-girls" are in short supply. If your measure for self-acceptance is how much you are praised, what happens when the praise stops coming?

Young or old, we are being driven toward perfection, despite the fact that perfection is a completely unattainable goal. We find ourselves reacting before reflecting, which doesn't generally yield the healthiest or wisest results. As a result, we live with too much self-doubt and too little self-health. It's reflected in a planet that is unhealthy and in a state of distress, from individual mental health to national economies to global environmental concerns.

When we are constantly looking for external validation and avoiding our own feelings, we become numb and aren't open to receive the gifts of life or even to see what is happening all around us. Don't get me wrong, as I understand and engage in the allure of a good merlot or a little retail therapy; but we need all things in

WE ALL NEED THINGS IN MODERATION

moderation. We need everyone to be fully engaged and aware of their surroundings because there's a whole lot of clean-up to do here. It is time to get the Alpha energy aligned and working in a purposeful way.

Whether you drink, smoke, overeat, or find yourself addicted to the Alpha lifestyle, it is a good idea to do a gut check and determine if you have actually fallen victim to these patterns.

As I said above, these things don't have to be a problem. Moderation is wonderful, and the whole point of this journey is to bring **Her** back into balance, after all.

MEDI-TATE, DON'T MEDI-CATE

Many of us experience the world as an amped and ramped, racked and stacked, hustling, bustling, droning beehive of information, appointments, broadcasts, paper-or-plastic?, noisy place. The Alpha Female finds herself easily sucked into the Frenetic Energetic due to her tendency to be pulled toward noise, distraction, and the race for success. This chaotic lifestyle of errands and PTO meetings, of pitches and lists and anything shiny, leaves little time for the Alpha Female to nurture herself. **Her** body is low on nutrients, and those long, sleepless nights begin causing strain. Next up are the migraines, the ongoing illnesses, and more.

These symptoms of dis-ease are often muted with the use of medication, numbing the body and blocking out the symptoms, but not necessarily fixing the root issue. The meds only do so much, and now you need to pull more dollars out of your wallet for a new medication or higher and higher doses. Or maybe you've determined the pills and prescriptions are not doing the job and are finding other ways to medicate while dealing with various side effects. Some of the most common methods of self medicating include using food, alcohol, social media, computer or phone screens, shopping, or sex to escape. For the Alpha Female, those means of self medication also extend to trying to be everything to everyone, as well as staying overwhelmingly "busy," yet still longing for more.

SELF MEDICATING SERVES AS A BAND AID RATHER THAN AN ACTUAL SOLUTION

They also take the power out of the Alpha when they're used irresponsibly or excessively. They limit the amount of time available for our minds, spirits, and bodies to heal, and serve only as a bandaid rather than an actual solution to the problems we face. What we need is to find mindful ways to Invoke **Grace** so we may rest and recharge.

This is where we call upon meditation. To many people, this word conjures images of deep breathing and feelings of calm. For the Alpha, though, the idea of someone sitting still and silent seems like nothing more than a big old waste of time. Both of these views of meditation can be accurate, and they can also be false. A wonderful aspect of meditation is that it is completely individualized. Sure, you can take a class or go on a week-long retreat, but you absolutely have the option to simply start small. That's what I did.

SIT IN THE QUIET MORNING WITHOUT JUDGEMENT AND WITH NO EXPECTATIONS

I started my practice of meditation with one itty-bitty, baby step: I woke up five minutes earlier in the morning. Just five minutes. With that tiny little chunk of time, I was able to simply lie quietly in bed while allowing thoughts to come and go as they pleased. None of those thoughts got to take center stage, though, as the payoff for this process was that my mind was able to sit in the quiet morning without judgement and with no **expectations**. For that first five minutes of the day, I let myself **Chuck the Checklist** and just be still.

The reason meditation is so important, even vital, for the Alpha Female is because it provides the opportunity to **Bring it Yin.** The focus is not on the external, the deadlines, the demands (self-imposed and otherwise), rather it is completely internal. Meditation invokes **Grace**, inviting it into the body that you are allowing to rest, restore, and replenish itself. My personal journey through MS cost me years of medication and tens of thousands of dollars a year on conventional therapies and insurance. It may shock you to learn that I was even a spokesperson and model for a drug company. If you happen to see an old MS pamphlet around, you might just see me with a big grin supporting the drug that supported me.

It may also come as a surprise that I still utilize medication to support my body as it combats the MS. I want to be clear in saying that I need certain meds and am not suggesting otherwise. After a yearlong hiatus, I have learned that the right ones are a blessing, and I currently take a different medication than the one in the pamphlet mentioned above. That said, it wasn't until I began meditating that I was able to hear my body's whispers and that I felt myself truly begin to heal. I could feel my body letting go of the symptoms of MS. My body became more mobile and agile. It felt more nourished and beautiful.

The point is that while medication serves a great purpose in fighting disease, it doesn't necessarily offer the kind of connective healing that works on the mind, body, and spirit. Meditation, on the other hand, helps you uncover and develop skills that can be used to become more grounded and healthy, as well as to find a place of **Grace** where dis-ease can heal. Moments of meditation give us the quiet space we need to celebrate progress over perfection and to find the joy that can reside in each of our cells.

MEDITATION CAN WORK TO NEUTRALIZE DEPRESSION AND ANXIETY

One of the important healing qualities of meditation is how it can work to neutralize depression and anxiety. It calms the mind, allowing you to **Get Out of Your Own Way**. The body responds to the relaxing meditative state, as energy shifts from a victim/bully mindset to one of gratitude. Of course, in more severe cases, such as autoimmune disease or mental disorders, meditation may need to work hand-in-hand with medication for optimal health and functioning. Those who choose meditation in this way may even find that fewer medications are needed or that doses can be lowered. That might not seem like much compared to a "cure," but we need to remember to seek **Progress, Not Perfection**.

If you have read the *Inspiring Grace* books in order, then you have likely already done some serious personal development. This requires a lot of diligent effort as you recognize and work with your **humbling blocks**. Believe me, sister, I know! Take some time to honor yourself for what you have accomplished. Praise your body for getting you this far, and do it a favor in return: meditate! In fact, if you have already set aside the time to read this, then you have a few minutes free right now to turn your thoughts inward. At the end of this section, put the book down, and quietly be wherever you are for five minutes. Don't forget to silence your cell phone to limit distractions. If you do it right now, you can feel the benefits immediately. If not, are you really going to do it later, or is it something that it will just get pushed out of the way again and again? This is an opportunity to give yourself a little healing and restoration, and it's not something you want to miss out on.

So, disregard what you may have heard in that online meditation tutorial you looked up once (with the best of intentions), and don't worry so much about doing it "right." Instead of stressing yourself out trying to block out your thoughts, allow each one to come to you and then be carried away like a bird in the breeze. You will also find a number of powerful mantras in the *Grace*

Guide that will follow this third book in the *Inspiring Grace* series. Feel your body in the chair, your feet as they connect with the floor. If silencing your mind isn't an option, try instead to picture your healthiest self. What does that person look like? How does she feel?

Before you turn the page, give yourself those few minutes and relish in the healing you are inviting into your body, mind, and spirit.

BRING IT YIN

Realistically, the nervous system isn't something we think about every day, despite the fact that it is quietly, efficiently, sustainably at work every moment of our lives. As an Alpha, you live the majority of your life in the sympathetic nervous system. This is where your body has the infamous "fight-or-flight" response. It's the thing that keeps us almost constantly on the defense. The sympathetic nervous system is like a knight who wears his armor all the time so that he is always ready to DO.

As we get the Alpha Aligned, life starts to shift more toward the parasympathetic. This is the part of the nervous system that allows the body to do its healing and rebuilding. Instead of "fight-or-flight," the parasympathetic is about "rest and digest." It's about "renew and restore." In addition to physical health, approaching the world through the parasympathetic helps to revive the spirit and rejuvenates the entire mind-body system.

In working with this **Ah-ha**, it is important to know **FIND AWE IN ALL OF YOUR BODY'S FUNCTIONS** how to access the parasympathetic nervous system. I suggest starting by taking a few minutes, perhaps in meditation, to contemplate your body. Find awe in all of its functions. Marvel at the sensation in your fingertips when they connect with an object. Enjoy the flexibility of your spine. Even acknowledge the twinge of pain in your neck when you turn your head to the left. This is how you **Bring it Yin,** and it allows you to sit with your body in a way that promotes what I call Help-Yourself Health.

Allow deep breaths to expand the lungs little by little. As they absorb more oxygen, it brings new life and increased blood flow that is healing at a cellular level. This type of restoration is momentary, as it takes but a few seconds to complete; but it is also an infinite resource, as most of us have the ability to engage deep breathing exercises at any time we so choose.

Most of us have no idea that we're spending the majority of our time in the sympathetic — that we're living in chronic stress where we aren't able to escape the otherwise useful state of fight-or-flight. When we remain here, there is no ability to self-heal. In fact, we generally expect our body to only rest during sleep (which we probably aren't getting enough of, either). We ignore the signs of dis-ease, even when we might know that our bodies are at their

WE IGNORE THE SIGNS OF DISEASE, EVEN WHEN WE KNOW OUR BODIES ARE AT THEIR TIPPING POINTS

tipping points. Instead, we slosh through our days feeling fatigued, often with head, back, and neck pain as part of the package. **Even when we recognize this discomfort,**

the Alpha nature wants us to push through it, to simply accept that everything is an obstacle to be overcome.

This forceful way of being takes a heavy toll. It becomes a catalyst that sends the body into constriction and convinces it to fight against us rather than working for our own benefit. It is in the spirit of the Alpha to persevere. This is in contrast to the spirit of the **Walk of Grace**, which is to seek calm and to focus on self-health. These are characteristics that align with those of the parasympathetic nervous system. When we drop into the parasympathetic, the body naturally begins to restore on its own.

Remember **Meditation, Not Medication?** Living in the parasympathetic can lessen the need for medication to drown out the pain, as muscles loosen, blood flows with ease to hydrate tissues, and that pain begins to subside on its own. The parasympathetic allows ease and fluidity. Like choosing the path of least resistance, the body finds it easier to work with itself. Life begins to flow back into the parts of the body that were tense and achy from living in a constant state of fight-or-flight. In the parasympathetic, we reside in a healing, balanced state where we are able to appreciate that which comes and release that which needs to go. We can be connected with Mother Nature and stand in awe of her beauty and power. This is where we wander with wonder as we contemplate the mysteries of life.

The transition from the **Frenetic Energetic** and the typical state of an Alpha frenzied by the external can be counterintuitive. Reaching a phase where we can rest, digest, and renew takes daily practice and mindful implementation of the Better-Than Plan. We have to choose to **Chuck the Checklist** and make conscious decisions to go soft instead of ramping up to full Alpha drive. My own impetus to take this path was the need to find a better way to combat the MS that shares my body. Considering the fact that it is my body, doesn't it make sense that I should get to know what's going on inside of it? More importantly, what things can I do for myself that no one else can? Again, this is Help-Yourself Health. I asked some important questions. What can I learn about myself to improve my health? How can I stay mobile when MS has crippled many others? I took a good friend's advice and made a point to listen to my body's whispers before She had to scream to get my attention.

SHE HAD TO SCREAM TO GET MY ATTENTION

What I needed to do was to **Bring it Yin.** When I paid attention, there was a lot to hear. My veins were resisting the medication prescribed for MS, for example. My body was telling me clearly enough that I needed a change. So, I took it upon myself to actively make mindful decisions that would keep me in the parasympathetic, to stay in that state where my body was able to better heal and rejuvenate itself. In my case, that included taking a self-prescribed drug holiday so that my veins could heal. To stay healthy during this

Western-medicine hiatus, I became very **intentional** with my energy. I chose my thoughts carefully so I was able to catch myself if I began to spin out.

It is most certainly not my natural condition to be soft and to lead from the heart. I practice each day in order to create and maintain this new normal. I pointedly nurture myself in mind, body, and spirit; giving myself permission and perspective rather than judgment. And should I begin to spin out, I turn to the **Ah-has.** To me, there is no better way to learn, heal, and love. So, I choose to **hold space** for myself when I feel particularly vulnerable, rather than making assumptions and judging myself. I remember that my goal is **Progress, Not Perfection.** In these moments I understand why it's important to practice these skills – or as I like to say, to dance the **Ah-has** – to train ourselves to be able to return to the **Ah-has** when we're struggling. I deeply understand at these times, that they are precisely what we need to move forward in **Grace.**

One technique I use to give myself permission to shift into this healthier mindset where I am a "Be-er" instead of a "Do-er" is to switch up the language when I meet a new person. It is common

GIVE YOURSELF PERMISSION AND PERSPECTIVE RATHER THAN JUDGEMENT

for our initial introductions to focus on Do-er questions. "What do you do for work?" "What do you like to do in your spare time?" These questions hold a person in the sympathetic, and when on the receiving end, they trigger us to amp up and justify why we are enough.

The next time you are in a conversation like this, I challenge you to answer these questions with the word, "Nothing." It will likely feel awkward at first, but it subconsciously allows you to be in the parasympathetic. It's an unexpected way to tell yourself that it is okay to not operate in **Alpha Overdrive,** that even if you don't have a million and one answers about what you do, it is absolutely enough to instead choose a state of self-healing. It may also make you **smile**, at least in hindsight, as you take the opportunity to break the **flow** in stagnant conversation that holds us in the sympathetic.

Instead of worrying about doing, you can instead enjoy simply growing your confidence in 'being.'

FAITH IT 'TIL
YOU MAKE IT

Wouldn't it feel absolutely wonderful to have everything in your life under control? For many of us, that's not a concept that we even consciously consider. Instead, we are stuck in "reality" where we often feel like we have absolutely nothing under control! How the heck do we find some sort of middle ground? My advice is to "faith it 'til you make it."

Obviously, this is a play on the phrase "fake it 'til you make it," but there are some important distinctions. Initially, I didn't like using the word "fake" because it seems inauthentic and, well, fake. That is definitely not a word that we like to use to label ourselves. In this sense, however, faking it doesn't mean that you put on a persona where you pretend that everything is perfect and nothing is wrong. It's not a call to refuse

CELEBRATE EACH HUMBLING BLOCK THAT YOU HAVE OVERCOME AND TRUST THE JOURNEY

help or to hide the real you from others. Instead of using such a loaded word, let's instead focus on the positive energy that **flows** when we have faith in our own selves. When I suggest an Alpha Female "faith it," I am advising her to go ahead and **get out of her own way**. I am encouraging her (you) to face your fears **faith-forward.**

It's time to go back and revisit that old friend and trusty **Ah-ha** that instructs us to **Get on the Better-Than Plan**. It requires us to celebrate each **humbling block** that we have overcome, trusting that each has been a wonderful part of the journey. Yes, there will be more difficulties ahead, but you've already shown yourself that you can face these things and still be okay. It's reasonable to have faith that you will do it again.

The other piece of this puzzle is setting and visualizing your goals. Maybe you aspire to be in a leadership position at work, but it hasn't happened yet. Putting yourself in the mindset of one who has that position (faith it) is one of the best things you can do to cultivate the confidence you need to actually attain that goal. Perhaps your goal is to do a headstand in yoga, but you have yet to make it a reality. Faith it! Put yourself in downward dog, put your head on the ground, and practice lifting each leg and doing a small kick up as if you were going into a headstand. Through visualization and practice, you will eventually get there!

I'm not just giving away advice here, I live this **stuff.** For eight years, I've been building my non-profit, *Underground Kindness*. For eight years, I've been moving forward without actually knowing exactly what I was doing or where I was going. It wasn't until this year that everything started to click in a way that finally felt right. I spent all that time moving toward something that I myself didn't quite understand. What I did know was that I had an outcome I wanted. Every day I visualized my goals and that would bring me further clarity.

At times, it has been downright terrifying. I dedicated my life, and most of my resources, to building something that brings value to self acceptance and self health. It's a lofty goal, but it's one that I have continually visualized, despite sometimes being scared as hell. This endeavor has required far more confidence than I really had. It would never have come to pass if I hadn't chosen the **Faith it 'Til You Make It** approach. Again, "faithing/faking it" doesn't mean pretending you're someone or something you're not. In the course of writing the *Inspiring Grace* series, for example, I do not pretend that I am an all-knowing guru whose words hold the secrets of the universe. Instead, I choose to authentically step forward as a person who has seen this applied wisdom play out in the mind-body, and I am here to inspire those who want to listen to my words. In

EMBODY AN UNCONDITIONAL ACCEPTANCE OF THE SELF THAT NATURALLY RIPPLES OUTWARD

an effort to lead by example, I try to embody an unconditional acceptance of the self that naturally ripples outward to become an acceptance of others who can then revel in their own radical self-acceptance.

If you have a calling or are driven by a passion but are also uncertain about how you will ever reach your goal, you need to bring your Alpha energy into alignment. Be patient with yourself and celebrate the victories, even when they're really small ones. If you need to, **Be Your Own Best Friend** and **hold space** when necessary. You have an amazing guide inside that is full of **magik** and power, and you also have the ability and the right to access it to become an Alpha on Purpose. It's a great way to bolster yourself when you're discouraged and to acknowledge your accomplishments when you're on a roll.

CALL ON YOUR COURAGE TO MOVE FORWARD AND YOU WILL TRULY SHINE

You have done a whole lot of work to get to this point. You've made it this far, and by calling on your courage to move forward you can truly shine, not just for the sake of being seen, but to light the way for others.

FROM WHY?
TO WOW!

How often do you find yourself suddenly pulled out of your own joy by another's attitude or actions? It's something that most of us deal with on a regular basis, and it's most definitely counterproductive to a **Walk of Grace.** This **Ah-ha** thwarts that interruption by moving our mindset from judgement to curiosity. It's about pulling ourselves out of the negativity before it has the chance to consume our time and steal away our joy. The trick is to shift **From Why? To Wow!**

This technique is pretty amazing as it keeps us aligned with our **Grace**. It protects us from slipping into **Alpha Overdrive**, which is likely to end uncomfortably for all involved. It is an effective means to keep from attacking someone else, as well as protecting us from our own judgement and self-ridicule after the event. When we ask "Why?" it is akin to opening Pandora's Box. The question leads to potentially limitless variables, the vast majority of which we just aren't going to like. When we question, we invariably start to judge, which leads to making excuses, and generally digging down deeper into things than is necessary, or even reasonable. In the end, all we've really done is upset ourselves while wasting precious energy that we could instead direct toward something productive.

WHEN WE QUESTION, WE INVARIABLY START TO JUDGE, WHICH LEADS TO MAKING EXCUSES

When we are faced with something new, instead of asking "Why?" it can also be completely acceptable to instead respond with "Wow!" and switch to a more empathetic approach to the situation. Rather than diving down a rabbit hole that will almost assuredly bring us to a place of irritation or frustration, the shift to "Wow!" allows us to skip the search for an answer, instead leaving a bit of a mystery and curiosity. It takes the other person from being difficult to being a means for expanding our own compassion. Not knowing the why of everything is a viable option, and it empowers us to reside in **Grace** and softness rather than choosing a journey that we're already pretty sure is going to cause physical and emotional anxiety, sending us into a state of dis-ease.

As an example, think of someone you know who perhaps likes to give out those backhanded compliments. You know, they probably say things like, "It's great that you can pull off that outfit. I just wouldn't have the courage to wear it." Your first reaction to that might easily be to wonder *why* you chose to wear that outfit. You might ask yourself *why* she wouldn't have worn it and if they are doing a double take when they look at you. You also might find yourself wondering *why* you pulled it out of the closet this morning in the first place.

The next time you're in a situation where someone does something along these lines, try going from **Why? To Wow!** Skip the whole

SKIP THE WHOLE PART WHERE YOU QUESTION YOURSELF AND YOUR CHOICE

part where you question yourself and your choice to wear your favorite look and instead think, "Wow! What is going on for her to feel like she needs to fill her bucket by dipping into mine?"

I find myself wondering what might be going on for that person that drives them to try and take someone else out of the game. This place of curiosity is so much healthier than judging the other person – or worse yet, yourself. It's definitely healthier than internalizing what has been said to you and turning to gossip. When we succumb to the petty anger and frustration, it is counterproductive and leaves us **Stuck in the Muck** over **stuff** that isn't even ours. They end up sucking you into the **victim vortex.**

It is important to stay in control of our emotions so that we can come from our softer side. It allows us to simply let things be rather than trying to force them into something that we want. Part of becoming an Aligned Alpha is realizing that just as we have chosen to get on The Better-Than Plan in an effort to become softer and lighter, others have the right to choose their own paths, too. Living out that understanding is easier said than done, but you can help yourself immensely by shifting from **Why? To Wow!** This small move metaphorically enables a protective forcefield around you; the projections of friends, foes, and family to bounce off. They can't gain purchase, sticking and sinking into your well-being. I like to say that going **From Why? To Wow!** is a step toward Invoking **Grace** via the High Road.

THE HIGH ROAD IS THE HEALTHY ROAD

We all know that the ideal in personal conflict is to be the bigger person, to avoid letting our emotions carry us away; but I'll be damned if choosing the high road isn't so hard! You don't always want to **Manage Your Own Stuff** or **peace ring** it out. It isn't as immediately gratifying to **hold space** for someone who makes a disparaging comment. Rather, you might just want to pounce on them like a predator on the Serengeti taking down a particularly impudent gazelle. It's so easy to go Alpha on a person who we feel has insulted or otherwise hurt us. At least temporarily,

IT'S SO EASY TO GO ALPHA ON A PERSON WHO WE FEEL HAS INSULTED OR OTHERWISE HURT US

it can feel really good to accuse, assume, label, and point fingers because this is how we reassure ourselves that we're right and the other person is wrong. We assert that "No, I'm not being defensive!" despite the fact that we're totally being defensive.

Although these books are not affiliated with any religion, I find a lot of value in the stories of Jesus Christ's walk through the world. He was this absolutely amazing being that somehow always managed to take the high road. People ridiculed, judged, and betrayed Him. Despite the many fingers being pointed at Him, He never pointed back. He didn't pick up the stones thrown at Him and cast them at His accusers. Again and again, He embodied a **Walk of Grace**, displaying His highest and healthiest self.

While you and I may not be pursuing divinity, His example still holds as we do reach toward a healthier level of our own existence. As you strive to ascend from **Recovering Alpha Female** to Alpha Aligned, you may very well find yourself judged and questioned by others. Frustrating as it may be, these interactions do provide an opportunity to practice staying true to yourself and your walk. Rather than attacking someone for questioning or misunderstanding you, you have the option to recognize that **The High Road is the Healthy Road.** Is it easy? Honestly, it's not. At least, not always. Once you're in practice, though, taking the high road actually provides a protection mechanism for you and your developing understanding of the world and your place in it.

YOU BEGIN TO RECOGNIZE THAT MANY OF THE FAULTS OTHERS FIND IN YOU ARE REALLY THEIR OWN SELF-DOUBT AND INSECURITIES

When you consistently take the high road, other people's judgements hold less and less ability to steal your inner joy. What **They** say rolls off of your fancy new teflon jacket and falls impotently to the ground. You begin to recognize that many of the faults others find in you are really their own self-doubt and and insecurities being projected outward. So much of the time when people criticize others, what they're really doing is pointing out the things they fear or lament about themselves. Fortunately for you, as you walk this path, you are shedding a whole lot of that self-judgement right along with your desire to condemn others.

Sometimes the high road feels really lonely and unfair, but it is one that you won't regret walking. This path is noble, as it requires both the strength to get there and

WHEN YOUR ALPHA ENERGY IS ALIGNED, THE VIEW IS CLEAR, ABUNDANT, AND EMPOWERING

the courage to stay. In the end, though, the rewards are boundless as our perspective shifts to give us a wider and deeper view. It's akin to the difference in perspectives between a ground-dwelling creature like a mouse and an airborne bird like an eagle. The little mouse is living in his **Frenetic Energetic,** scurrying about and only seeing what's right in front of him as it pertains to survival. The eagle, however, has a much more encompassing view from his home in the sky. The mouse burrows in the grass while the eagle floats along. In addition, the eagle sees far more than the mouse, and yet, he is unaffected by the majority of it. In my mind, that is true mastery. When your Alpha energy is aligned, the view is clear, abundant, and empowering.

Consider these concepts from the perspective of parenting. Sometimes our children seem to be out of control, and as a parent it's not uncommon to feel unsupported, judged, and possibly even thwarted in your response. It's natural for us to be triggered by the negative energy of the moment, but it is so important for us to offer our **Youngers** the unconditional love that is necessary to sustain them through their self-discovery. I like to say that it's important for us to love them through the ugly (it's also necessary to love yourself through the ugly, by the way). Just as we are striving to accept ourselves, so, too, are they. The perspective from which we approach their struggle has an incredible impact on how we feel about ourselves, as well as how they end up seeing themselves. When we step back and see the larger picture, and also choose options like moving **From Why? To Wow!,** for example, we end up giving an important gift to the child, but also to ourselves.

A lot of times, the high road leads us to discover new territory. The Alpha Aligned possesses the strength and courage necessary to get to this new, wondrous place, and she is primed to see and appreciate the magnificent view.

ALPHA UP

In this book, I've spoken of the mindset where one is a Be-er instead of a Do-er. This harkens all the way back to one of my favorite quotes from the first book that says "Being is just as much a verb as doing." Throughout this series, I have encouraged you to welcome **Grace**, quiet, and reflection – to be soft. Now is the time to finesse the skills you have practiced and incorporated in a way that brings both your true Alpha spirit and your hard-won **Grace** into balance.

So there is no confusion, I want to reiterate what I've said in the past: Alpha energy is awesome. Being an Alpha Female can absolutely be a strength, not to mention a blessing to those around you. We need Alpha energy on this planet! She is the one who wrote these books. She is the one who had the tenacity to move the nonprofit forward, rather than escaping to her rose garden or using her time to **Feng Shui Her Day** away. That said, we also have to give the Alpha within us the space and permission needed to become aligned with **Her** softness. It's absolutely vital to our physical, emotional, and spiritual health. And if the Alpha energy is a blessing to others, it's in everyone's best interest for her to be healthy and happy, right?

ALPHAS BRING MUCH NEEDED DRIVE, SPIRIT, AND GUSTO TO THE WORLD AROUND US

We Alphas bring much needed drive, spirit, and gusto to the world around us. To paraphrase the comedian Tina Fey, "Alphas get stuff done!"

What we don't need, however, is more burnt-out, overwhelmed women who are so concerned about doing everything "right" that they do so at the expense of their own well-being. When you are the embodiment of Alpha energy, you will always be most productive when living primarily in your place of Grace. The bulk of your time should be **Getting Certain with Uncertainty,** for example, rather than trying to exert influence and control on everything around you. Instead, you can call upon the skills you need only when necessary, thereby building yourself a far more peaceful life.

My personal experience is currently smack dab in the middle of this lesson. I know that it is time to put these books out into the world in order to build momentum for the *Inspiring Grace* movement. If I were to live only in my place of Grace, it would be easiest to simply sit back and hope the movement somehow makes its way into the mainstream. After all, putting it out and expecting myself to drive it forward sounds a bit like **Expectation is Resentment in the Making,** because I want something for and from this work. I want it to reach into the hearts of Alpha Females and help them recognize the need to be softer, to give themselves **Grace**, and to choose self-health.

Sitting back and patiently waiting for the "perfect moment," however, is not what is needed. Alphas need this movement so they may feel encouraged and supported in their walk; and they aren't going to get that unless I Alpha Up and work to transform my ideas into concrete actions. This is a time when it is right to move outwards and upwards instead of solely turning inward. The key to it is to ground the actions I take in power rather than in force. I can use my powerful Alpha energy to make a difference in the world without slipping into the old mindset that I need to force my ideas on others so I can feel like I have succeeded. When we Alpha Up, we incorporate all of the skills we've developed throughout this series so that we can stand in the light to authentically and naturally attract what we need.

To that end, I choose **Fluidity, Not Rigidity.** I accept the need to **Chuck the Checklist,** to **Forget the Fairytale,** and to notice when I get **Stuck in the Muck**. It's time to put these things forward without **expectation** or pushing for a specific outcome. I will allow the power of the ideas to **flow** rather than utilizing my energy to try and force them onto others.

When I need to remember to balance Alpha and **Grace**, I use the analogy of the Mama Bear. We all know the scenario where Mama Bear goes into Alpha mode when she believes that her cubs are in danger. She muscles up for a fight to protect her loved ones. She knows how to Alpha Up! Once the threat has passed, however, she does not stay in Alpha mode. She's not out there picking fights with every ground squirrel and whitetail deer that she thinks is looking at her cross-eyed. Instead, she drops back into her place of motherhood and Grace where she harvests berries and plays with the cubs she adores.

Just like Mama Bear, it is not feasible to always walk in **Grace**, any more than it is helpful to constantly remain in fight-or-flight mode. Instead, we move back and forth between the two as needed. We should remember to **Bring it YIN,** remaining **Predominantly Parasympathetic.** We know that we've got the ability to **Alpha Up** when the situation calls for it.

VICTIM VORTEX

Just for a moment think about a recent Disney or Hollywood movie that you've seen. Can you identify the main character types in each film? Most likely, there is someone needing to be rescued. Whether the movie is for children or adults, a major plot point likely revolves around a person or group that has been oppressed, trapped, abused, or misunderstood. A common theme would be the "damsel in distress."

In addition to the character who is helpless and hopeless, you'll probably also find their nemesis: the bully. They're the ones who do the oppressing, trapping, and abusing. The victim and the bully suffer a toxic relationship wherein they feed off one another until another common character comes along. It's the hero to the rescue! This person steps in to save the day with their good deeds and positive attitude. They get themselves involved in other's business because they have a deep-rooted need to help. In fact, heroes often feel compelled to help others even when they seem unable to help themselves. What we end up with is an endless cycle of movie characters who are the victim, the bully, and the hero.

THE NAME DOESN'T MATTER AS MUCH AS THE AWARENESS OF THE TOXIC RELATIONSHIP CYCLE

This is a pattern called the **Victim Vortex.** It's likely I chose that name because I often find myself falling into the role of the victim. If you happen to embody a different role, you could possibly make this **Ah-ha** more personal by calling it the Hero Hurricane or the Bully Blizzard (that's the best my thesaurus could do on that last one...). You will possibly even find that you switch roles as you travel around the **Victim Vortex** again and again. The name doesn't matter so much as does an awareness of the toxic relationship cycle we have been conditioned to suffer as far back as when we fell in love with that favorite childhood movie.

Within this vortex of negativity, constriction, self-ridicule, and dis-ease, there is no **Grace** and no power. It's impossible to operate from a place of Grace while residing within this triangle. It is called a vortex because it brings you down and keeps you disempowered. As long as you're playing your role in the vortex, you're distracted from all the other wonderful ways you could be. Instead, we end up in one of the corners where we are paralyzed by fear and disallowing. If you look at the graphic, you can see that there is a triangle that is surrounded by gifts. Those gifts are available to you as soon as you are willing to step off the ride around the vortex.

In thinking of it this way, as a vortex that one travels around, we find that it pertains not only to ourselves, but also to those who join us there, either willingly or because we have pulled them in. We suck others into our vortex when we try to play the hero, thereby casting them the victim. Likewise, we may relegate them to the role of hero whose job it is to rescue us.

The **Victim Vortex** isn't just some abstract idea, either. Much of our modern life is set up in a way that keeps us in a powerless vortex. We ride that triangle all day long in countless different scenarios. Consider how our systems of medicine, education, government, law, or insurance are designed in just this way. This usually translates in such a way that we small individuals are defaulted into the role of victims while the large-scale operations bully us into needing a hero – which they also "conveniently" provide. It's not even completely our fault that we ride around this triangle without giving it a thought, as we have long been conditioned to do so.

The first step in being able to get off the ride is to recognize that you're on it. As they say, "Awareness is the key to change." Once you realize which corner you are in

THE FIRST STEP IN BEING ABLE TO GET OFF THE RIDE IS TO RECOGNIZE THAT YOU'RE ON IT

naturally, then you can make your move and exit the ride. It is easier said than done, I know. The best motivating factor, though, is that once you jump off the **Victim Vortex,** with its contradictory characteristics of chaos and futility, you are free to enjoy the bountiful rewards that are on the outside.

When I was able to step out of the role of victim (as someone with MS, as a single parent, as the mom to a child with learning challenges), I received the gift of empathy for both myself and others. I was also able to take what I had learned during my time in the victim corner of the vortex and transform it from a burden into a gift. My experiences had taught me about perseverance and introduced me to my favorite mantra, "Keep on keepin' on." Now I can use these skills not to simply survive victimhood, but to actually rise up as a victor on my own terms. In my case, I apply what I have learned to my daily life with MS. Instead of letting myself fall victim to my symptoms, I use them as motivation to participate actively in my health and wellness.

A version of this exists no matter which corner of the **Victim Vortex** you exit. If you've spent time as a bully, for example, you have insight into both the need and the means for compassion toward others. Rather than remaining a bully or overcompensating by recasting yourself as the victim, you instead have the opportunity to humble yourself and understand that we are more efficient when we work together instead of against each other. This is where we learn the gift of collaboration over competition.

The hero role has always been interesting to me. We see the hero as the "good guy," so how could playing the hero be a bad thing? Well, when we cast ourselves as the hero, we naturally place others into the role of victim and/or bully. We are lauding ourselves as stronger, smarter, and more able to help someone than they are to help themselves. In addition, the hero is often the person who just cannot help but to take the weight off of others and put it onto her own shoulders. In doing so, she is jeopardizing her own health and opening herself to resentment. In short, it is disempowering to both sides of the relationship. Once the hero steps off of the triangle, they are able to learn about self-acceptance. External validation and applause becomes less necessary, and the person has the opportunity to learn that it is enough to be your own hero. They are now free to engage in their own life and self-health rather than being more concerned with the business of others (remember to **Manage Your Own Stuff** from book 2).

When I realize I once again need to get off the **Victim Vortex**, it always helps to refer back to wisdom already won. For me, this often means remembering to **Be Your Own Best Friend.** We tend to stay in the vortex because that's where everyone else is, because when you feel like a victim, you expect a hero to find and save you. I noticed this tendency when I started to take the power back from my MS. Instead of being a victim in need of rescue, I was prepared to be my own hero. I also found

IT IS CRUCIAL FOR YOUR SELF-LOVE AND SELF-ACCEPTANCE TO COME FIRST

that I received fewer offers from others to play the hero role for me. It was obvious that I was able to fill that role myself. Talk about empowering!

Remember that it is crucial for your self-love and self-acceptance to come first. When you have that kind of strength, it creates a light within you. And since like attracts like, you find yourself among positive, healthy people with relationships that transform into something lighter and brighter than you've experienced before. When we're in the triangle, we are caught in a vortex where we are disempowered, debilitated, and **Stuck in the Muck.** Once you have the strength to step off and onto your own two feet, however, you open yourself to balance and stability. Just like at the amusement park, the ride might be fun for a little while, but you certainly wouldn't want to live like that.

MOVING FROM DISEMPOWERMENT TO
Empowerment

UNCONDITIONAL ACCEPTANCE

Awareness

RESCUER

BULLY

POWERLESS

VICTIM

GRACE

EMPOWER-MENT

VICTOR

VICTIM VORTEX >>> CREATION ENERGY

These are the gifts I discovered for me. Each of us will have our own experience and gifts. The key to stepping into your own power is to: Notice which corner you gravitate to, own and acknowledge the feeling, and switch your mindset to allow empowerment and self health.

CATALYST VS CREDIT

Everyone out there is looking for some sort of credit. Consider the students who put in the most work on their group project, or the homemaker who cleans up after everyone while keeping them fed, bathed, and loved. Whether it's cultural or intrinsically human, we all seem to want credit for our efforts. Think about yourself and what kind of credit you may seek from your boss, spouse, or acquaintances. If you really break it down, what we call "credit," is often simply acknowledgement. It boils down to a sense of being appreciated, of being seen or heard.

I, myself, can recall so many occasions in my personal experience where I wished to be recognized for the non-profit organization that I manifested and built, for the jobs that I provided to community members. I saw so many people becoming their own bright lights as a result of my mission, and I wanted credit for igniting that light. I didn't entirely appreciate the idea that I was simply giving myself away for free. Didn't I deserve kudos for the hard work, the money, and the years of effort that I contributed to a dream with an unknown outcome? Even if it wasn't in the form of a direct "thank you," it still felt so good to be appreciated and recognized for my efforts. Not only did I desire that credit, I also felt resentful when I didn't receive it.

It took some time, but I did realize that Walking in **Grace** is its own reward. Doing good leaves me feeling full of light, and that is certainly more rewarding than a plaque and a pat on the back. Although it feels good to be appreciated, it isn't strictly necessary. It is okay to simply revel in the fact that I have inspired others to grow within themselves, just as I have grown from the efforts of my mentors, **Youngers**, and friends. They have been catalysts in my life, and I am able to be a catalyst for others. This is the Love Loop in action!

Seeing yourself as a catalyst and pursuing the desire for credit definitely stirs up some contradictory feelings. Of course, the Alpha **YOUR OWN SELF-WORTH AND ACKNOWLEDGEMENT REALLY IS ENOUGH** Female wants credit, as external validation is key for her. As we strive to become aligned, though, it's time to dismantle our need for others to see and approve of what we do. Instead, practice the skills you've been learning throughout this series. In the case of **Catalyst vs Credit,** one of the more helpful **Ah-has** is the one that directs you to **Be Your Own Best Friend**. Give yourself an "atta' girl!" and know that your own sense of self-worth and acknowledgement really is enough. When you "get" that, you remove the opportunity for resentment to sneak in and wreak havoc. What a wonderful superpower to have!

There is nothing quite like the sense of standing on your own two feet. It is empowering and beautiful. When you stand unabashedly in your own radiant light without the need for an audience, you expand your self-confidence and ability to set and maintain boundaries. In short, you become your healthiest self, full of tenacity and authenticity; all the while exuding creative energy. It is from this perspective that you can inspire others even more so than you did before. Not only that, but you will also find in the long run that other people naturally become more grateful, creative, and motivated than they ever would have if you'd pushed and prodded them to praise your hard work.

In this way, true gratitude and support ripple into the world without the need for fear or force. When you stand in your light, accepting its unique beauty and strength, your example encourages others to give themselves permission to stand in their own light, as well. In this culture of productivity, we need more heart than head to fuel passion. If you can be a lustrous glow, an inspiring beacon to guide others to do the same, you can be a catalyst for creating leaders rather than competitors. There is far more than enough fighting for fame, which is often just another name for credit, going on all around us. What we really need is partnership, collaboration, sisterhood, and support. Together, we are undeniably stronger. The credit might present itself as a natural outcome, but what we learn is that being the catalyst is an important role of service and value.

WHAT WE REALLY NEED IS PARTNERSHIP, COLLABORATION, SISTERHOOD, AND SUPPORT

When coming from a place of Grace, it is easier to understand that credit is only one of many types of rewards. The source of those other rewards isn't always as direct as getting a top billing or having your name on a certificate of achievement, but when you give wholeheartedly, the world returns your love in plenty of unattached and unassuming ways.

Few of us want to show up somewhere to do the work and receive no credit. If you are operating from a purpose-driven place, however, there are many ways to interpret just what that means to you.

GIVE NOT TO GET

Catalyst vs Credit is the one **Ah-ha** in this book that has its own entire subsection. I hope that clarifies for you just how important it is in your **Walk of Grace**. To that end, let's drill down even deeper into the concepts above.

As is likely a part of the human condition, we generally give to others with an unspoken **expectation** that we will receive something in return. When we do something for someone else, we await something in return – even if it is on a subconscious level. Perhaps the reward will be material, such as in the form of payment or exchange for goods or services. It might also be physical, or even verbal. In the end, it is presumed that if we give, we will in turn collect our dues.

Why do we seem to resent the idea of giving freely, with no **expectation** of some sort of compensation? It actually stems from the cultural stigma that is the bartering system. You give money and get an item; you give a **smile**, you get a **smile**. It's all about the quid pro quo. When we give without receiving something in return, it confuses us. It can upset us so much that we are less likely to give in the future. After all, we know that **Expectation is Resentment in the Making,** and this is a perfect example of when that resentment comes knocking at the back door of your generous heart.

As we gain a deeper understanding of **Grace** and the role it plays in our minds and bodies, we can recognize how it resides in giving. When you take the burden from another or offer kindness for its own sake, that is **Grace** manifested. To do what is right for you with no **expectation** of a reward is to allow your actions to stem from your own confidence and a pure place of service. You are strong, fearless, and full of love. You have plenty to give and do, whether or not there is a direct reward for your actions.

You also understand that there are different types of rewards, many of which arrive unbidden and in utterly unexpected ways. Maybe your kindness won't be repaid directly, but the concept of Karma tells us that what goes around, comes around. If you give freely, whether or not the recipient offers thanks or compensation, life still provides you with free and unattached abundance that **flows** to you in ways that are completely unrelated to the service or good deed you performed. Give good, get good.

When the Alpha is aligned, she finds value simply in who she is. Acting as a catalyst for change has led to sometimes overwhelming generosity in my life, for example. After understanding that seeking credit is an unproductive use of my time that can leave me full of resentment, I made a conscious effort to stop looking for it. Instead, I opened my heart to a surplus of gifts, both tangible and intangible, as well as to the pure love that the world has to offer. When we stop chasing, we finally hold still long enough for wonderful things to find us.

The Alpha has a genuinely generous heart, but it is often overshadowed by a false sense of humility. I think that many of us can secretly relate to the idea that we want to receive,

THE ALPHA HAS A GENUINELY GENEROUS HEART

but we absolutely don't want to admit to it, let alone to ask for it. The brilliant thing is that you don't need to rely on others to receive. This is the time for you to notice the areas in your life where abundance is coming to you in ways that don't seem directly related to the energy you put out. Do you have good health? A flexible work schedule? Fantastic eyesight? Competent, reliable children or a faithful partner? These things aren't direct rewards for the way you give to and serve others, but don't doubt that they are related. You might not be able to draw a straight line from an action (giving) to an influx of abundance (receiving), but one is derived from the other in the grander scheme of your experience on this planet.

DIS-EASE TO PLEASE

The previous concept is closely related to the **Dis-ease to Please.** This ailment is part and parcel in the journey of the **Alpha-holic.** A hallmark of the Alpha Female is her drive to work hard in order to achieve success. She dearly hopes that her success is enough that **They** will be impressed and fill her empty reserves with recognition and validation, not to mention paychecks and promotions. She relentlessly seeks this assurance of her worth through religious affiliations, book clubs, or the PTA, but most of all her career. She pushes herself to the limit, bringing her to the starting point for dis-ease, pain, constriction, and likely a generous helping of self-deprecation. Despite the risks, the Alpha Female will continue to work extra hard in an effort to appear as the best version of herself in hopes of being accepted and regarded as noteworthy.

This constant exertion of physical and emotional energy sends the body right into **Alpha Overdrive.** Note the difference between consciously choosing to Alpha Up from a calmer, softer place and going into **Alpha Overdrive,** which means ramping up even further

ALPHA OVERDRIVE IS UNSUSTAINABLE

from that already **Frenetic Energetic. Alpha Overdrive** is unsustainable, although we will certainly push to our very limits in an effort to make it last. We will gather all the forces we can to make sure that **They** are impressed, glossing over the fact that this kind of energy is only healthy when it is mutual.

We've already examined the idea that we should **Give Not to Get,** and that the rewards received from giving are often not what we expect or even associate with what we have given. As you choose this **Walk of Grace,** however, it is always important to design a life that is balanced. One-sided energy where you expect yourself to only give, give, give is what I define as the **Dis-ease to Please**. In my view it is precisely that, a dis-ease.

The dis-ease aspect comes into play because the constant output of energy takes a toll on the body. Operating in **Alpha Overdrive** pushes the body to unhealthy limits. Physically, your body is a ball of tense muscles with restricted blood flow to the organs. A mind with dis-ease often follows suit and creates a body with dis-ease. You may even find you suffer from palpitations that are nervous and irregular.

Recognizing the **Dis-ease to Please** was absolutely pivotal for me in my journey with autoimmune disease. When I focused so much of my energy on pleasing others, I redirected it away from its more important purposes, such as keeping my body healthy. The tendency to "people please" puts so much extra weight and stress on our shoulders, not to mention physical weight, because our actions are dedicated to generating happiness for someone else, rather than for oneself. Stress, depression, anxiety; these are only a few of the symptoms of the **Dis-ease to Please** and are caused by our dire need to be accepted by others. It is undeniable that people will go to extreme lengths for love in its many forms, including positive attention. We have a wealth of literature and film devoted to that very concept.

When we work to align the Alpha and switch to **Grace**, we are striving to move from the external to the internal. We realize that the reward of giving can be the giving itself, which is something that comes from within. Of course, the reward could also be receiving, and while we don't want that external source to be the be-all, end-all, we also do want to recognize its place in a healthy cycle. Give, receive. Give, receive. This is how we picture a mutual, healthy exchange. As we discovered in Book Two, "It is in giving that we receive and in receiving that we give." It is the ultimate Love Loop! It is no coincidence, then, that when we allow ourselves to receive, we are simultaneously providing someone else with the gift of giving. Each of us is able to fulfill our Love Loop because it requires an exchange, rather than a one-way **flow**.

When the Alpha female is aligned, she no longer performs for an audience, but for her own spirit. She gives to others, and if she isn't reciprocated with an equal amount of effort from the recipient, she can set aside time and energy to reward herself. As we saw above, rewards for our deeds and actions can come to us in ways we never expected. One of the places it can come from is our own selves. When you are willing to fill up your own love cup, you replenish your own energy and service your own needs. When this is possible, your service to others comes from an authentic place of **Grace** where you know your own needs. You know when to give and when to refrain from giving because it is at your own peril. It can be so hard for an Alpha to draw lines between what she is and is not willing to do, which is why I remind myself and others that **Boundaries Aren't Bitchy.**

BOUNDARIES
AREN'T BITCHY

This particular Ah-ha incorporates the **Power in the Pause** – which we'll be exploring next – with the need to **Manage Your Own Stuff,** as well as several other of the *Inspiring Grace* techniques that we have been practicing with the help of time, commitment, and lots of self-love. **Boundaries Aren't Bitchy** empowers and softens at the same time. This duality is in line with our ultimate goal to find balance in the Alpha Female, to become Alpha Aligned.

It's not unusual for the Alpha Female to be a leader in her family and a contributor in her community. She is a role model for her children, and the life of the party at ladies' night out. She most definitely has high **expectations** for herself. When you look deeper, however, you find that many of those **expectations** originate not from her, but from other people's views, opinions, and demands – what **They** think. Friends, family, and colleagues expect you to fulfill certain duties and wishes simply because you always have. You don't want to let these people down, because external accolades are what the Alpha thrives on.

I am a pleaser who doesn't like conflict, so you can imagine how much I struggle to honor this **Ah-ha.** Remember that I am not an expert or guru, rather I am here to inspire light and spread love, while supporting and enjoying as I journey on. I find it extremely difficult

I FIND IT EXTREMELY DIFFICULT TO PUT UP BOUNDARIES FOR MYSELF

to put up boundaries for myself. When I do choose to assert myself and set these limits, it feels intimidating at the onset. After the awkward part is done, a wave of relief slips over me and the stress dissipates. How often do you attend functions even though you're annoyed and frustrated that you agreed to go in the first place? Setting boundaries and making better choices can help you remove this feeling from your life, which is certainly a good thing for your own personal development. It also sets an example of honoring oneself, plus giving others permission to do the same.

Constantly trying to keep up with other's **expectations** is too much. It puts the already busy mind and body into **Alpha Overdrive,** with all of the hardships that particular frenetic state of being brings with it (you can review that information in *Book Two, Inspiring Grace*). Rather than being an **Alpha-holic,** the goal is to become aligned with our Alpha, to find balance within **Her** that overcomes the "need to please" and refocuses our energy on much more important things like your own health, happiness, and love.

BECOME ALIGNED WITH YOUR ALPHA AND FIND BALANCE WITHIN HER

Putting up boundaries isn't bitchy. It's so common for friends and family to **volun-tell** you to do something, to sign you up for another responsibility, or to assume that you will contribute just because it's what they expect, in part because it's what you've always done. If you want limits, it's time to recognize that other people are absolutely, 100% not going to set them for you. Why would they suddenly decide to protect your time and energy rather than benefiting from it? People are used to getting all they can from you because you have endorsed this pattern, and you're the only one who is going to be able to change that. You *need* to set boundaries for yourself, and you *need* to be okay with it, and accept that *it's not bitchy.*

This isn't just about adding some free time to your schedule to read a book or get sucked into a new series on Netflix, rather it's about your health. Self-health, self-care, and self-preservation all go hand-in-hand! All of the hard work you're choosing through this series and will continue with the follow-up *Grace Guide* is helping you work toward that self-health. Each step you take toward emotional and spiritual **Grace** is providing your body with space to relax and drop into the parasympathetic where it can heal itself. When you realize just how much your physical health can benefit from slowing things down and even (gasp!) saying "no" to requests, those things start looking like the rational choice to make.

Setting boundaries is an opportunity to express your opinion and then have your own back even when the process feels a little harsh or rough around the edges. Remind yourself that you are coming from a place of **Grace** and love, and make a point to offer yourself the unconditional acceptance that we seek from others.

POWER IN
THE PAUSE

If you've ever heard me advise to get comfortable with awkward, then you'll recognize that this is the **Ah-ha** that can help get you there. After all, when you take a moment to **pause**, it leaves an unfortunate amount of room for the awkwardness to sneak in and pitch a tent. At least, that's how it tends to feel. We are so used to filling the dead air with noise and movement that a silent **pause** can feel desperately uncomfortable. So, we talk at dinner, we talk over coffee, we talk to our seat mates on airplane rides and to strangers in elevators. The Alpha, she likes to talk, and she struggles with silence. What we forget is that when we cease the talking, the empty space that's left provides wonderful opportunities for authenticity to come forward.

When we consciously insert a **pause** in our daily trip through life, we are able to open ourselves up to a great many wonders and heart whispers. One simple, although not always easy way to enable this **pause** is to practice

**EXAMINE
WHAT IS BEING
COMMUNICATED**

taking a ten-second break during conversations. This break in the momentum provides a number of benefits, even if it does feel a little uncomfortable at first. For example, that **pause** can give your mind a moment to **Reflect, Not React** to what your conversational partner is saying. Those ten seconds afford you an opportunity to examine what is being communicated to you so you can understand it instead of just opening your mouth and saying the first thing that comes to mind. We all have so many decisions to make daily, and it is nearly impossible to answer every question that comes your way with absolute certainty.

Often times in parenting, you find that your kiddos want an immediate answer to their questions. When faced with these kinds of urgent, and often complex demands for action or requests for permission, it's not uncommon to simply mutter "sure" without thinking, or likewise to deny permission with a "no" that wasn't actually well thought out at all. These answers aren't necessarily based in what makes sense or is appropriate in the situation, rather they are default responses sent to the mouth by a brain that is too distracted to process the request. They also leave you feeling unnecessarily defensive.

That's not to say that you aren't distracted for completely logical reasons. All parents know that patience is not most children's strong suit, so their timing is less about what works and more about what they want from you right this second. Once you put out that knee-jerk "sure" or "no," however, it becomes exceedingly difficult to take it back after you've had time to reflect and realize you should have given it a minute. A simple way to defer making an immediate decision about something that requires a bit of thought is to replace those instantaneous "sure" and "no" answers with phrases like, "if you need an answer now, it's no," or even "no, for now" or "let me ponder that." This builds in the **pause** you need to examine the facts and make a more informed decision. It gives you a little time and a little wiggle room, too.

On other occasions, the Alpha is so busy that she gives an immediate answer without thinking or, ahem, signs up to help a friend or co-worker out when she really shouldn't have. We've all done it, and we've all regretted it. These moments become so awkward and stressful that they create a whole new layer of unnecessary strain in what is already obviously a very busy, distracted life. Again, you can circumvent much of this self-induced stress by utilizing the above phrases. "Let me ponder that," "give me a moment," or "no, for now." You are invoking the **pause** that you need to take a deeper, smarter look at the situation and take in the bigger picture.

Utilizing the pause is akin to the more rhyme-y, catchy phrase, "Check yourself before you wreck yourself!" By putting a little space between now and the need for a well-thought-out answer, you give yourself time to examine the request from a more intellectual standpoint; and you can also let your body have some input so you make a decision based in **Grace** rather than mindlessly responding from the **frenetic energetic.**

By operating from the Alpha Aligned, we offer ourselves alternative, flexible answers. The purpose of the pause is to provide that chance to reflect rather than react. It is how the Alpha stays authentic. It's how she implements choices mindfully and with love and understanding instead of falling back on the old methods of using/responding to fear and force. There is so much **Power in the Pause.** It gives you a chance to truly listen to what others are saying and then to answer only after the kind of contemplation that leads to gentler, more loving, and Alpha Aligned decisions.

Pausing in this way is one of those things that has to be practiced. It doesn't come naturally to the Alpha to muster up the Grace to walk away from a request so she can get quiet and seek an authentic response. It's ingrained in us to simply pop out an answer on the spot and then have to abide by whatever happened to come out of our mouths. When we do remember to hit pause by saying, "No, for now," or even "Give me a moment," we develop the skills needed to become more graceful and evolved when dealing with tough questions in the future. If you need support for the "No, for now" motto, refer back to your other *Inspiring Grace* books where you will find guidance in **Ah-has** such as **Go With Your Gut.** Like any other **Ah-ha,** it's all about the **Better-Than Plan:** doing a little better today than we did yesterday, and preparing to enter tomorrow with a bit more **Grace** and self-awareness.

TIRED AND TENDER

This particular Ah-ha was inspired by a dear friend of mine who not only loves my Alpha, but also needs my Omega when she is feeling tired and tender. I always try to offer proper respect to the Alpha side of my personality, as it is and has been invaluable in my life. It's wonderful to befriend an Alpha who will help you set your goals, motivate you to accomplish them when you're sluggish, and remind you of your dreams when you seem to have forgotten them yourself. But sometimes, when we are worn out from the day or the week or the year, we just need someone to listen and give us permission to do nothing. The Alpha isn't generally the person you'd want to seek out for this role. At least, she didn't used to be.

My sincere hope is that you've been able to encourage your **quirky** friends to join you on your journey. It is so wonderful to have a few Alpha gal-pals who are aware that an amped and ramped personality may come across as harsh or forceful, and are therefore willing to meet us on a different level when we just need someone to **hold space** for our weak and unattractive moments. When you are each seeking the kind of transformation offered through the *Inspiring Grace* series, there's a wonderful opportunity to support each other in an **intentional**, compassionate way. This union of understanding across friends can establish a magical tribe full of love and support that you've likely not experienced before.

Another Recovering Alpha Female can act as sort of a **"processing partner."** Finding a person to fill that position is such a gift. It feels amazing to have someone who will love you up when you need it. When that person is also on her own **Walk With Grace**, she is able to support you when you need it rather than veering into **Alpha Overdrive** and demanding that you "buck up, buttercup" or presenting you with a list of all the ways she can fix it for you. In this new walk, it is exceedingly valuable to have a friend who is willing to motivate you, but who is also willing to simply love you through the ugly. It is just as important to be that friend, both to yourself and others, so you can support each other to simply "be" rather than to "do" all the time.

When you can come from this soft, tender side of the Alpha, your actions are loving, and your empathy is genuine. Rather than trying to force your friend, or yourself, to move in a certain direction, you can just accept the person

BELIEVE THAT THERE IS CLARITY AHEAD

where they happen to be. Better yet, you can hold them tightly while they're there. When you begin the *Inspiring Grace* journey, it is unlikely you will really know what lies ahead. Instead, you must trust the way, and even if you don't quite know how you'll get there, believe that there is clarity ahead. **Be Your Own Best Friend** when you need to, and **hold that space** for yourself as you travel through the unknown.

Developing this type of understanding is the heart of what it means to listen instead of assume. It's learning how to accept rather than to force. As we do this for ourselves, we naturally become more empathetic and compassionate toward others. We are able to blossom into the type of friend who listens as well as who inspires. In the long run, that is a much more empowering friend to have and to be. It is okay to be vulnerable or tired or sad. Vulnerability is not a character defect, rather it is precisely the thing that makes it possible to explore our inner selves as we seek **Grace**. Expressing when you're tender allows those around you to do the small things they can to **hold space** and to fill your love cup when you are too tired or raw or self-loathing. Sometimes, what that looks like is simply sitting and listening, as you give yourself permission to do nothing but be tired and tender.

ORGANIZE,
DON'T AGONIZE

First I told you to **Feng Shui Your Day.** Then I advise you to get on the **Better-Than Plan.** Now I'm here to encourage you to **Organize, Don't Agonize.** I like to group these three **Ah-has** together because they are each about making small steps toward clarity. At the same time that they teach us how and why to declutter our physical space, they also offer insight into how and why we can do the same for our minds.

We all have the moments where we sit in judgement of ourselves. We're fuming over how messy the closet has gotten (again) or that the Halloween/Christmas/Birthday party decorations are spilling out of their boxes and taking over the garage (also again) in a disorienting and somewhat desperate display of holiday spirit. It's hard not to feel like a failure when the things that seem like they should be so easy somehow remain out of hand, but residing in judgment truly is such a waste of your time and energy. The goal here isn't to add more shame or to get down on yourself for getting down on yourself, rather to recognize that self-bullying offers absolutely nothing productive or joyful to your life.

LITTLE BITS OF PROGRESS IN THE PHYSICAL WORLD CAN HAVE A PROFOUND EFFECT ON THE EMOTIONAL ONE

Instead, try using the moments you would have spent berating yourself to instead organize one small thing, like a box or a shelf. Your time is so much more well spent organizing than agonizing, don't you agree? When you take that moment or two to clear up some of the mess you see in front of you, it naturally results in clearing away some of the haze that is fogging up your mind. Little bits of progress in the physical world can have an absolutely profound effect on the emotional one that resides in each of us.

For example, I was frustrated with myself because I had six boxes of *stuff* that I need to sort through. They sat there and mocked me and encouraged my brain to tell me all kinds of nasty things about myself. Finally, I had to stop agonizing over what I would do with the **stuff,** how I would find the time to take care of it, etc. and just start organizing. So, I consolidated those six boxes into two. Did that get the job done? No, it didn't. But if I don't take on the mentality that I just need to start, then I will continue to sit there immobilized because the project seems daunting and overwhelming.

This is actually a technique that is commonly used by survivors of life-threatening diseases. Oftentimes we are so tired, strained, and overwhelmed that we feel like we just don't have the bandwidth or capacity to take on large tasks. Getting started, doing small chunks, getting on the **Better-Than Plan,** these are the things we can do, even when we can't do everything. As a result, there's a new sense

THERE ARE THINGS WE CAN DO, EVEN WHEN WE CAN'T DO EVERYTHING

of accomplishment, too, that helps to chase away the negative, hateful things that try to convince you you're less-than. It is so important on this journey of recovery from the Alpha life that we remind ourselves of the need for **Progress, Not Perfection.** Seriously, give yourself a win and some peace of mind by just taking small steps toward organizing and accepting that it's okay not to get it all done at once.

Remember not to be afraid to ask for help!! Find a friend who finds joy in tidying and decluttering and invite them to help you. You don't have to do it all. It can make all the difference in the world to get their outside perspective.

HERE AND NOW

Lover Not a Lifer

Speaking for myself, but also from the shared experience of many others, I have drawn the conclusion that when it comes to intimate partners, security is a top priority for most women. This isn't hard to understand, whether from a cultural or a biological perspective. Oftentimes, though, we get so caught up in our concerns about the future and what kind of security resides there that we end up living our present moments in fear instead of trust.

Personally, I found myself thinking about my financial future with my partner after we hit some **humbling blocks** in our own relationship. That line of thought brought up feelings of fear, rather than those of faith in what is to come. I started worrying about what I would do if something were to happen to him, or me, or us. My partner shone a spotlight on the situation, revealing a harsh and honest reality when he set his own boundary. He told me that if I wanted to be with him, I needed to be with him "here and now." He needed me to be in the present with him where we currently did have security, rather than fixating on the future and its lack of guarantee. This is where I came up with a reframe in my mind to help me through the pain. I hatched the concept

Lover, Not a Lifer. This ironically empowered me in our partnership and allowed us to be together enjoying the here and now.

It took some time but I began to realize that instead of placing my feelings of security in someone else, in an unpromised future with them, I needed to be providing that security for myself. No matter what happens in life, I'm always going to have me, so maybe that is a reasonable place to find the things I need. When women find the strength to be secure in themselves, magical things seem to happen. In fact, it often results in our many fears and financial concerns turning themselves around for the better.

Living in the **Here and Now** does come with risks, one of which is losing that **perfect-on-paper** life that we Alphas have so meticulously groomed. It requires us to gather our newfound understanding of how

LIVING IN THE HERE AND NOW TAKES THE PRESSURE OFF OF YOUR ROMANTIC PARTNER

to **Forget the Fairytale;** to be willing to let go of the picture we have of a perfect life with a perfect partner, sipping the perfect wine in our perfectly tended gardens. That image of an unattainable fairytale life takes us right out of the 'Now' and puts all of our precious energy into trying to be certain about the uncertain future. Talk about setting ourselves up for failure! Beyond the temporary **magik** of the fairytale, it provides no opportunity for the

Alpha Female to stand solid in her own light, power, and self-security.

In addition to regaining your personal power, functioning in the **Here and Now** takes the pressure off of your romantic partner. This can be scary, as many women live in fear that they will lose their partner if they loosen their grip on that person. In the real world, however, I have found the exact opposite to be true. Loosening the grip allows the other person to show up in their own **YOUnique** way while you **Hold Space** for their personal expression. This form of acceptance from the Alpha empowers the partner rather than manipulating or trying to control certain situations, appearances, and behaviors. So liberating for both!

If you take the pressure off your romantic partner, they become free from what they may have previously viewed as a burden or nagging from you. They want to give you the love you desire; they really do! This can happen best when they aren't being suffocated by the Alpha's tight grip on their life and choices. That behavior only closes the Love Loop. Try this little exercise for a deeper understanding. It helps immensely if you literally hold your hands up and follow the thought process here:

Place your hands together in front of you, as if in prayer. Now, pull them about three inches apart, keeping them parallel, and pretend there is a magnetic push between the two. Your right hand is you, the left is your partner. When you (right hand) lean in, your partner (left hand) starts to lean away. The further you bend your hand toward the other, the more you close off that space between them. It almost looks as if you are shutting a door. There simply is no room between the two for love and energy to **flow** freely. The same is true when you go the other way. Both hands end up in awkward positions, causing discomfort and rigidity. Start again, adjusting both hands back to the original position where they point straight up. When you look at them in this position, you can see that they are in harmony, with neither one pushing or pulling. This represents balance in the relationship where the **Love Loop** is open to give and receive freely.

If you are able to keep this in mind during trifling times, it inspires your partner to do the same. When they see that you are supportive, that you appreciate their efforts, it excites them to give, to **hold space,** and to show love more liberally. In the spirit of balance, the **flow** goes both ways. You are both empowered and authentic. The love is so much sweeter and more rewarding because both sides feel at ease and loved in their honest expression.

This is, by far, one of the most challenging **Ah-has** I currently face. When you feel yourself start to go Alpha on your partner, remember to shift **From Why? To Wow!** From this perspective, it can be easier to remain curious and stay engaged.

SHIFT FROM WHY? TO WOW! TO GAIN NEW PERSPECTIVE

Remember to treat yourself as kindly as you desire your partner to treat you. Take a bath, massage your feet, or buy yourself flowers. This brings you back to recognizing that your security lies within yourself, not within someone else, resulting in self-confidence and an easing of angst.

Not only does **Here and Now** remove the stress of worrying about the future of your relationship, but it also provides the opportunity you need to be the full, freely-giving lover that you want to be with your partner right now.

READY TO RADIATE

Through daily practice of the techniques offered in the *Inspiring Grace* series, the Alpha Female is able to grow bold and colorful in her own self. **Her** authentic voice becomes powerful in its truth and self-security. Now, as **She** starts to unfold, empower, and self secure, there is a natural tendency for **Her** to use this new power for good and living a life **Grounded in Grace.**

An example from my own experience goes back to the nonprofit organization I founded, *Underground Kindness.* I was amped and ramped and wanted to fling myself at the project because I was so inspired by the possibilities. I wanted everyone else to be invigorated by the movement and was spurred further by knowing it was something aimed at our **Youngers,** that it could usher in a softer, kinder next generation. I was deep into the "save the world" mentality, moving into **Alpha Overdrive.** My intentions were pure, honest, and good in wanting to inspire **Grace** and unconditional acceptance. But I have found that the true inspiration comes when I am walking the talk.

Eventually, the movement took its own course, and it is now freestanding with a board and funding and everything else that I had hoped for in those early days. The thing is, all of that didn't come about because I pushed and wore myself out. It all ended up happening in its own time and in its own way, in part because I was able to let go of controlling expectations. Losing myself to the Alpha was not only unnecessary, but unhealthy.

USE THE GRACE YOU'RE LEARNING TO TEMPER YOUR EXTREMES

As an Alpha, is it vital to use the **Grace** you're learning to temper your extremes. **Grace** is what keeps the spirit charged and grounded. And that takes us back to daily practice of the techniques and a dedication to self-health. It's certainly okay to Alpha Up when it's warranted, but only when it is warranted. Call upon the **Ah-has** to **Be Your Own Best Friend,** to recall the importance of **Progress, Not Perfection,** and to allow light into your life as you **Get Out of Your Own Way.** Remember, we're trying to **Bring it YIN** and live **Predominantly Parasympathetic.** The work in these three books is difficult. It is emotional. It is also the best difficult, emotional work I have ever done for my overall health.

As you find yourself growing stronger in your walk, you will also find that you're **Ready to Radiate** passion and bravery. Your fresh, courageous outlook will come alongside a plethora of opportunities that are now available to you. Being able to radiate that energy without going into **Alpha Overdrive** is the perfect test for your new sense of balance. Remember that when you are **Ready**

to Radiate, you will also be offering inspiration rather than information, and your message will come without fear or force.

In yoga, the warrior series resonates with the Alpha. Strength, agility, and focus are what holds your body in position. As you shift to Mountain, though, you are able to **Bring it Yin,** without sacrificing that strength. Tell yourself again and again: There is strength and grounding in **Grace**.

Understanding like this comes in handy in all kinds of scenarios. In corporate settings, for example, you should be striving to communicate in an authentic way that is powerful, but doesn't require the use of force to get what you want. To do this well, you have to be able to stand firm and have your own back. No matter where you are, scenarios that you would have previously found difficult or intimidating become less intimidating when you remember that your bright light is something to share and shine. Let your light shine the way, rather than to be seen. This will inspire others. You are ready to take on unfamiliar or intuited tasks because you are bold and brave. Remember to temper your Alpha ways to remain empowered and grounded. The light you share is a soft glow, not a thousand-watt bulb. Your light inspires but never blinds. This is how you lead from **Grace.**

The Alpha is a do-er. This we know. Now is the time to listen to your heart whispers, to be the light. You are ready, you are strong, and you are balanced. You are your own Woo-Woo guru for your mind, body, and spirit. As you ignite your light, and choose inspiration, not information, you will live a colorful, creative, and fully expressed life.

FAILING FORWARD

As I near the conclusion of the *Inspiring Grace* trilogy – a few years, many milestones, and countless lessons from where I started – I am learning to fully live and appreciate the faith, future, and beauty of **Failing Forward.** In true entrepreneurial style, I wake each day to face the unknown. I cannot say what the forthcoming years hold for my business, not to mention my health or my love life. Anyone who has followed their heart knows that such a pursuit comes with a lot of floundering.

This Alpha movement is alive and full of energy. It is gaining traction. I am aware that it could easily slip from my grasp should I allow myself to be distracted by the uncertainty and insecurity that I feel while outside of my comfort zone. I am able to monitor my self-doubt, to see when it is arising to stir fear in my heart. We Alphas rely on the external accolades, and when we have an unusual calling in life – one that maybe not everyone "gets" – we can easily fall victim to the idea that we are too vulnerable and alone. It's not always easy to **Be the Black Sheep.**

Rather than residing in fear, however, I am finding that the very techniques I'm sharing with you work to keep me humbled and strengthened by the unknown. I am able to trust in the universe or whatever that thing is that is greater than I, while also relying on the ideas presented in Book One, *Recovering Alpha Female*, under **Go With Your Gut.** It serves as an ongoing call to stay empowered by the **YOUnique**, vibrant, feminine spirit that is inside of you just as much as it is inside of me.

I absolutely have a lot of questions about my future. When I try to envision myself guiding the *Inspiring Grace* movement, I see plenty of question marks. Rather than letting this detour me from the **Walk With Grace,** however, I accept that there are unknowns and choose to **Get Certain With Uncertainty.** I see this as a chance to rejoice that I've been able to dance every single step of the **Ah-has** in order to build the strength and path needed to face the unknown **faith-forward. Failing Forward** isn't a degradation that implies all we can do is fail, rather it is a reminder that when we do fail, it is not the end of the world. In fact, failing is one of the things that helps us move forward on the unfolding journey of life. We Alphas need to **hold space** for **humbling blocks** so we can accept them for what they are. Then we can pick up the pieces knowing that we are traveling in the right direction. We can be guided by our intuition as we invoke **Grace** on the planet. Each of us starts with our own community, and the ripples **flow** unforced outwards from there.

FAILING FORWARD IS A REMINDER THAT WHEN WE DO FAIL, IT'S NOT THE END OF THE WORLD

This concept of failure is not always easy to grasp. It really requires us to **Cultivate Confidence** in a careful way, potentially refining our approach over years that will undoubtedly include struggle, triumph, failure, and success. It comes down to having the faith needed to keep on keepin' on. For me, that is accomplished through authentic connections in relationships where I lovingly accept myself and recognize the many colors in others. This is why I continue to champion the cause of unconditional acceptance through these books and *Underground Kindness.*

NOURISH TO FLOURISH

If you look closely, you'll realize that everything I've shared with you throughout this entire series has one unifying factor: It's all about the concept of breaking old beliefs and accepting new ones that will better serve your spirit. When you change your thoughts, the new way of being ripples outward, raising you to be your healthiest self and even positively impacting those you encounter, and potentially those *they* encounter! Making that change is a matter of exploring the ideas and using them as techniques to live a balanced life as your healthiest self. Even though Alphas tend to be direct and can come across like a blowtorch,

LIVE A BALANCED LIFE AS YOUR HEALTHIEST SELF they are full of love and more than willing to give their energy to people and causes they care about. Just remember that in order to maintain authentic and healthy relationships with others, we need to wholly and unconditionally make that connection with ourselves first.

In more familiar terms, it's just like putting on your own oxygen mask first when caught in an emergency. When you take care of yourself first, all of the other things become so much more realistic. Help-Yourself Health starts and ends with nourishing your whole Being. If you want to be a brighter version of yourself, you can. You need to love the body you're in, feed healthy thoughts to your mind, and give your spirit the authentic voice in your life. When you make a commitment to doing these things, you become more open to receiving, and it will seem as if gifts are just presenting themselves from out of nowhere. Of course, everything doesn't change in a day. Your family relationships aren't going to immediately transform into healthy connections simply because you set a few boundaries, for example. But setting those boundaries is exactly what is needed to open yourself to receiving the gift of healthy relationships. One paves the way for the other.

Everything doesn't change in a day, and change isn't permanent, but when you nourish yourself, you can take on the world in a much more positive way. Nourishment isn't just about eating healthy foods and taking vitamins, by the way. Don't get me wrong, putting those good things into your body is crucial, but it needs to be done in combination with the other **Ah-has**. Synergy is such an important part of your **bekomming**. Just as food nourishes your body, the **Ah-has** serve as nourishment for the mind and spirit. All of this works together to fulfill you and guide you to your own **Walk of Grace.**

Nourishing yourself is remembering that when you have one finger pointed at someone else, there are three more fingers on your own hand that are pointing back at you.

WHEN YOU HAVE ONE FINGER POINTED AT SOMEONE ELSE, THERE ARE THREE MORE FINGERS ON YOUR OWN HAND THAT ARE POINTING BACK AT YOU

It is the breath of life that sustains you when breaking old habits, halting the addictive personality, and benching the Alpha so this sweet, kind, **Graceful** being can take **Her** place. The beautiful, feminine energy that **She** embodies is where love lives. When old habits are broken and dis-ease begins to subside, you will feel yourself flourish in life. You will be open to receiving the gifts that the world has to offer you and can accept them without limits or **expectations**. The shift into **Grace** will absolutely change your life forever.

Epilogue:

TRUSTING YOUR JOURNEY

Thank you so much for joining me on this journey, and congratulations on taking your own **Walk of Grace.** I'm fully aware of how much work these **Ah-has** can be. Every day I find myself dancing through them for mastery. While it can be fun to work through them in order, it's also good to note that each is there individually when your situation warrants it. It's totally reasonable to pick and choose the technique that fits a given situation.

For example, let's say you've spent some time encouraging yourself to **Faith it 'Til You Make It** and have been feeling good about your results. What happens when there's an upcoming family get-together where you will have that faith tested, where others will spend time undermining your growth by pointing out past failures or making snide remarks that make you feel like you are never good enough? Well, it sounds like a perfect time to go back and learn how to **Be the Black Sheep.** It might also be useful to refresh yourself on the finer points of the **Victim Vortex** while you're at it! The point is, you now have a whole cornucopia of skills and suggestions to draw from in order to stay the course you choose for yourself.

One of my favorite practices for staying in the right mind space during my **Walk of Grace** comes from a teacher I had many years ago. You may know the acronym WTF. It's descriptive and powerful in its own right, but I want to leave you with another view of it. In my world, those three letters stand for "Where's the Focus?" When you find yourself scattered or struggling, maybe even asking yourself "WTF, man?" reframe your question. Remember to bring your focus back to where it belongs so you can **Cultivate Confidence** in your own Walk.

When you arm yourself with the skills and techniques in the *Inspiring Grace* series, you'll be far less likely to fall into your old pattern. Instead of having them triggered by someone else's old patterns of behavior, you can now find new, better, more sustainable responses that change the outcome of interactions. Physically, emotionally, and spiritually, dancing the **Ah-has** can help you better manage and even abandon dis-ease by replacing it with self-health. The true result is that long-sought sense of inner peace. This is how you Invoke **Grace**; it's how you become an Alpha on Purpose.

If you'd like to go deeper with the **Ah-has** and how to implement them effectively in your life, the follow-up *Grace Guide* will be a wonderful tool for you. This workbook will take you through the entirety of the

Ah-has from the series, providing action steps you can take to truly live the life you've been wishing for. However you plan to move forward, I just want to remind you (and then remind you again), that you can do this! You can learn to put the Alpha in her place, so that she works for you instead of the other way around. You can uncover and nurture that softer side where so much feminine energy and ability to love reside. You can **hold space** when things need to simply sit and be, and you can also Alpha Up when a situation calls for that kind of short-term intensity. You truly do have this all within you, and each step you take will bring you self-health as you move ever closer to acceptance and **Grace**, trust the way, and even if you don't quite know how you'll get there, believe that there is clarity ahead. **Be Your Own Best Friend** when you need to, and **hold that space** for yourself as you travel through the unknown.

Developing this type of understanding is the heart of what it means to listen instead of assume. It's learning how to accept rather than to force. As we do this for ourselves, we naturally become more empathetic and compassionate toward others. We are able to blossom into the type of friend who listens as well as who inspires. In the long run, that is a much more empowering friend to have and to be. It is okay to be vulnerable or tired or sad. Vulnerability is not a character defect, rather it is precisely the thing that makes it possible to explore our inner selves as we seek **Grace**. Expressing when you're tender allows those around you to do the small things they can to **hold space** and to fill your love cup when you are too tired or raw or self-loathing. Sometimes, what that looks like is simply sitting and listening, as you give yourself permission to do nothing but be tired and tender.

Learn More About Lindy's Vision

THE NEXT CHAPTER

Let Your Color Out:

Supporting and inspiring overachieving women to walk a little softer, appreciate the moment, and embrace their colorful quirks. Let Your Color Out is a for-profit company designed to inspire unconditional self-acceptance and hold space for transformation while empowering women to step fully into life, living colorfully and out loud. **www.lindylewis.com**

Underground Kindness:

A non-profit organization, presenting Compassionists into the classroom to introduce young people to the practice and philosophies of stress reduction and mindful living.

Underground Kindness creates a learning environment that is free of judgment, expectation and competition. **It is our vision to encourage and nurture the 'whole student,'** through compassionate, all-inclusive classroom programs, such as: Anti-Bullying, Stress Management, Authentic Relating, Creative Journaling, Relationships 101, Yoga, Meditation, and Team Building, to name a few.

Our goal is to provide classes and workshops that support the growth of our teens into self-reflective, expressive, happy, healthy members of society. Students who are offered opportunities to relax, develop self-awareness and practice interpersonal skills, are more available for learning, are more willing to share their talents, and through compassion for self, are able to ripple that back out into their world: family, friends and community.

ALL UNDERGROUND KINDNESS CLASSES ARE FREE TO STUDENTS AND THE SCHOOLS!

We are supported 100% by the generosity
of grants and donations.

KINDNESS IS CONTAGIOUS...

For more information please visit:
www.undergroundkindness.org

ABOUT THE AUTHOR

LINDY LEWIS – Lindy spent most of her adult life as a working woman in Corporate America while raising three children and adeptly managing an autoimmune disease that impacted not only her body, but also her spirit. Lindy's Perfect on Paper lifestyle crashed hard when exhaustion, fear, and stress became overwhelming and she realized that life had something entirely different in mind for her. When her fairytale marriage came to an end, it launched a transformation. Her life opened to a variety of healing modalities as she focused on letting go of expectations and self-judgement.

Through this empowering process she utilized a series of constructive Ah-has to maintain her health and live a life of possibilities. In her books she transforms the diagnosis of Multiple Sclerosis, single parenting, and Being the Black Sheep into a gift of self-health.

LINDY'S LINGO
TO LIVE BY

Throughout the *Inspiring Grace* series, RAF retreats, peace rings, speaking, yoga, and more you will find a number of terms entitled "Lindy Language." These are helpful linguistic shortcuts that convey many very meaningful concepts. To that end, each of the books includes a "glossary" of words and phrases that you are encouraged to incorporate into your head space as you start to take your own **Walk with Grace.**

Book 1

RAF (Recovering Alpha Female): One who chooses to soften and allow her beautiful feminine spirit to unfold, transform and inspire.

Ah-ha: Pivotal moment launching transformation.

Compassionist: One who holds a place of Grace and compassion for self and others.

Feng Shui: Organization energetically – creating flow, freedom and happy places.

"Her": The woman who wants to live authentically, honestly and with more intention.

Hold Space: Patience and an honoring of your transformative process.

Humbling Blocks: Those moments in our climb that take us out of control and mess with our plan.

Let Your Color Out: Acknowledging and accepting one's quirks, and then giving them expression.

Munay: Nourishing, all-encompassing love.

Perfect on Paper: Just that! – on paper!

Processing Partner: That person you can be totally raw with and still feel acceptance, as well as listening as you find your way through the feelings.

Selfish: Learning to be more like yourself.

"They": Collective Consciousness; Society; them, everybody… family and friends that define our decisions.

Underground Kindness: (Lindy's non-profit) A quiet movement to bring balance to Public Education by presenting Compassionists in the classrooms, and introducing stress management tools, mindfulness techniques and unconditional acceptance to our Youngers.

Walk of Grace: That place of being in the bullseye and aligned where you accept all that is.

Woo-Woo: The crazy stuff, that works.

Woo-Woo Guru: Beautiful souls that choose (daily) to practice unconventional wisdom, energy management and trust in their knowing.

Youngers: These brilliant young people, our children, that teach us each day with their honesty, joy, and living from the heart.

YOUnique: Celebrating your authentic self and appreciating your true nature.

Zen Zone: That place of stillness we can go to when the noise of the world takes us out.

Book 2:

80HD: The way my son heard his ADHD diagnosis; now a reminder that each beautiful brain interprets so YOUniquely.

Alpha-demic: A woman who has thrown herself into her schooling with the goals of external validation and good grades; potentially overshadowing the joy of learning and the value of knowledge gained.

Alpha-fall: Frequent relapses where one forgets to stay in the flow and present; lets self doubt creep in, often leading one to be 'stuck in the muck.'

Alpha-holic: We are who we are. The Alpha-holic is one whose overarching, solution-driven, multitasking personality seems innate within her. It can be a beautiful thing, but she also needs to soften herself and guide her energy purposefully.

Alpha Overdrive: The natural 'Type A' speed; steamrolling ahead with no real regard for opinions or reflections; usually exhausting.

Black Sheep: Previously considered a misfit or viewed in a negative light, the RAF owns and embraces those things that differentiate her from her family, colleagues, or peers.

Expectations: Resentment in the making.

Faith-forward: Trusting your knowing; choosing to move fearlessly in the direction that inherently calls on a gut level; dharma.

Flow: A beautiful experience when one is so engaged in something fulfilling that it seems to literally flow from a higher plane.

JOMO: Joy of Missing Out.

Magik: Magik in the moment; embracing what's to come instead of fearing it; in this place of unknown is where the magik happens.

Momentfulness: Being really present, aware, and engaged only in what is happening to the point that distractions hold no power; leaving one clear and focused.

Pause: Space; the pause has great power.

Quirks: Colors or peculiar behavioral habits that comprise aspects of an individual's character and personality.

Smile: A glow of Grace upon one's face.

Stuff: Not only physical belongings, but also the thoughts, emotions, values, and expectations one holds.

Volun-tell, Volun-told: When one person "volunteers" another for a job, task, or to do something; forcing involvement without asking.

Zenter: To bring yourself back into balance; to plug in to your authentic self and recharge.

Book 3:

Bekomming: Evolving into your healthiest and highest self, often by holding space and loving yourself through the ugly, thereby morphing into your "selfiest" self.

Code Blue: A predetermined way to call for help from one or more friends, family members, etc. when you find yourself down or stuck in negativity with the intention to help pull you out of your funk through kind words, a care package, or some other positive form of attention.

God-ism: The little miracles that happen every day, but that we might normally overlook. Examples might include hitting all the green stoplights, unexpectedly finding exactly what you're looking for, and even being "in flow." Be on the lookout and celebrate them when they appear.

Individuating: What happens to a Younger when they start to do their own bekomming. It sometimes involves, breaking from your "group" and feeling awkward in order to get to your authentic self.

Intentional living: Staying curious and living in possibility. questioning conditioning and making different choices.

Magi: Living 'the more.'

Hot Mess: Instead use: wild spirit; crazily creative; fiercely passionate; intensely intuitive.

Mind Maze: A kinder word for monkey mind; allows for creativity rather than scattered and unpredictable.

Self-Health: Practicing each day to use the guide inside to heal, create and dream in your bekomming.

Self-Reference: Looking within to find answers, listening to the heart whispers.

Sistering: The carpentry term for when one board is too weak, to come up alongside of it for support and to offer support, strength and power.

Souls Journey: Your purpose, and how you listening to your own wisdom to pursue and realize it.

Underthink: As an alpha we tend to overthink everything. Practice under-thinking situations as we waste our precious energy spinning out!

Zen-den: A physical space you can create for yourself where you feel safe and creative. Your own "nest."

Printed in the United States
By Bookmasters